SPEECH PREPARATION

WORKBOOK

SPEECH PREPARATION

WORKBOOK

Jennifer Dreyer
San Diego State University

Gregory H. Patton
San Diego State University

PRENTICE HALL, Englewood Cliffs, NJ 07632

© 1994 by **PRENTICE-HALL, INC.**
A Paramount Communications Company
Englewood Cliffs, N.J. 07632

10 9 8 7 6 5

ISBN 0-13-559569-X
Printed in the United States of America

Contents

Audience Analysis

Audience analysis can be defined as the process of examining information about the expected listeners to a speech. This analysis helps us to adapt our message so that our listeners will respond as we wish.

The following pages will allow you to practice analyzing different audiences. You will also learn how to adapt a speech to a particular audience.

Demographic Analysis

Age   Gender

Religion   Culture, Ethnic, and Racial Background

Education   Occupation

Socio-economic status

Attitudinal Analysis

Is the audience interested in or apathetic about your topic?

If the topic is controversial, is the audience for or against it?

What is the audience's attitude toward the speaker?

Environmental Analysis

What are the physical arrangements for the speaking situation?

How will the seats be arranged?

How many people are expected to attend?

Will you speak from a lectern?

What time of day will the speech be delivered?

Demographic Analysis Worksheet

Name_____   **Instructor**_____

You will be giving several speeches to the other students in your speech class over the course of the semester. Using the demographics outlined on page 1, take some time to analyze your classmates.

1. Average <u>age</u> of the students: _____

2. <u>Gender</u> composition: _____

3. What are the different <u>cultures</u> represented in my class?

    _____

4. What different <u>religions</u> are represented in my class?

    _____

5. What is the <u>education</u> level of the students? (e.g., is it all freshmen or are there juniors and seniors in the class?)

    _____

6. Occupation: Do the students work? If so, where? (The answer to this question will help you to determine their socio-economic status below).

    _____

7. Socio-economic status: _____

Did you find some of these questions difficult to answer? It is likely that you will. If you need more information about the individuals in your class, ASK THEM QUESTIONS or have your instructor ask questions to determine the demographics of your class.

Use this analysis as a reference for the rest of the semester. Be sure to review it before preparing and delivering <u>each</u> speech.

Audience Adaptation Exercise #1

A sample speech topic and brief excerpt from the speech are provided below. Read the excerpt and then determine how you, as the speaker, would need to adapt the speech based on the audiences listed below.

Topic: Traffic Congestion

Thesis Statement: Traffic congestion is a major problem for America today.

It only seems to get worse! Each day as I drive to work I encounter more cars on the freeways. The dangers to our environment are tremendous. With all of those cars on the road, we are polluting our air and destroying the earth's ozone layer. And that's not all! The congested traffic increases the risk of getting in car accidents. My sister was in three accidents in the past year while driving to and from work in Los Angeles.

Audience:

Rural farmers who travel to the city about once every six weeks

Adaptations I would make:

_____

_____

_____

_____

Audience:

Young couples moving to Los Angeles to find work

Adaptations I would make:

_____

_____

_____

_____

Audience Adaptation Exercise #2

A sample speech topic and brief excerpt from the speech are provided below. Read the excerpt and then determine how you, as the speaker, would need to adapt the speech based on the audiences listed below.

Topic: Dieting

Thesis Statement: Losing weight is difficult for most individuals.

The battle of the bulge! For many people, this is one of the most difficult struggles in their life. How many of you have dieted before? How many have dieted five or more times? For a diet to be successful, it needs to be a lifestyle change, not a one week or one month "change." Losing weight is not only about giving up some of your favorite foods, it's also about exercising. Exercise raises your metabolism and makes it possible to lose excess weight.

<u>Audience</u>:

A group of overweight teenagers attending a "How to Diet" seminar

<u>Adaptations I would make</u>:

_____

_____

_____

_____

<u>Audience</u>:

A group of nutritionists at a local hospital

<u>Adaptations I would make</u>:

_____

_____

_____

_____

Audience Adaptation Exercise #3

A sample speech topic and brief excerpt from the speech are provided below. Read the excerpt and then determine how you, as the speaker, would need to adapt the speech based on the audiences listed below.

Topic: Immigration

Thesis Statement: Immigration has had a significant impact on the United States.

Half of the growth in the United States population is due to immigration. New immigrants arriving in this country bring with them rich cultures and traditions. In addition, they provide unique contributions and ideas to American society. New immigrants, however, are also the target of hatred and resentment, often by people whose relatives were immigrants themselves.

Audience:

Unemployed workers meeting at the local unemployment office

Adaptations I would make:

_____

_____

_____

_____

Audience:

A group of new United States citizens

Adaptations I would make:

_____

_____

_____

_____

Conducting an Attitudinal Audience Analysis
Speech #1: _____

Use the following page to analyze the audience for your first speech.

You will probably want to refer to the **Demographic Analysis Worksheet**, which lists the demographics of your classroom. Use this page to analyze the audience's attitude toward your topic and you, the speaker.

Attitudinal Analysis

1. Do the students in your class have an opinion about your topic? If so, what is that opinion?

    _____

    _____

2. Is the audience interested in or apathetic about your topic?

    _____

    _____

3. Does the topic directly affect your classmates? If so, how?

    _____

    _____

4. What is the audience's attitude toward you, the speaker?

    _____

    _____

5. How does your topic relate to the other speeches scheduled to be delivered?

    _____

    _____

If you don't know the answer to some of these questions, ASK YOUR CLASSMATES QUESTIONS and use page 9 of this workbook as a guide.

Conducting an Attitudinal Audience Analysis
Speech #2: _____

Use the following page to analyze the audience for your second speech. Remember, your audience will have different feelings about each topic you present.

Attitudinal Analysis

1. Do the students in your class have an opinion about your topic? If so, what is that opinion?

   _____

   _____

2. Is the audience interested in or apathetic about your topic?

   _____

   _____

3. Does the topic directly affect your classmates? If so, how?

   _____

   _____

4. What is the audience's attitude toward you, the speaker?

   _____

   _____

5. How does your topic relate to the other speeches scheduled to be delivered?

   _____

   _____

If you don't know the answer to some of these questions, ASK YOUR CLASSMATES QUESTIONS and use page 9 of this workbook as a guide.

Conducting an Attitudinal Audience Analysis
Speech #3: _____

Use the following page to analyze the audience for your third speech. Remember, your audience will have different feelings about each topic you present.

Attitudinal Analysis

1. Do the students in your class have an opinion about your topic? If so, what is that opinion?

    _____

    _____

2. Is the audience interested in or apathetic about your topic?

    _____

    _____

3. Does the topic directly affect your classmates? If so, how?

    _____

    _____

4. What is the audience's attitude toward you, the speaker?

    _____

    _____

5. How does your topic relate to the other speeches scheduled to be delivered?

    _____

    _____

If you don't know the answer to some of these questions, ASK YOUR CLASSMATES QUESTIONS and use page 9 of this workbook as a guide.

Gathering Attitudinal Information

How do you go about developing a formal attitudinal survey?

Your first task is to decide what you want to know about your audience that you don't already know. Once you have made that decision, you should next plan the questions that will give you this information.

There are two basic types of questions:

1. Open-ended questions: questions that allow for unrestricted answers, without limiting answers to choices or alternatives.

2. Closed-ended questions: questions that offer an alternative for an answer, such as true-false, agree-disagree, or multiple choice questions.

Exercise

Suppose that you plan to address an audience about **television violence**. What questions would you create to gather more attitudinal information?

What are three open-ended questions you might ask?

1. _____

2. _____

3. _____

What are three close-ended questions you might ask?

1. _____

2. _____

3. _____

Conducting an Environmental Audience Analysis
Classroom Worksheet

1. What are the physical arrangements for the speaking situation?

    _____

    _____

2. How will the seats be arranged?

    _____

    _____

3. How many people are expected to attend?

    _____

    _____

4. Will I speak from a lectern? If not, will I have anything between me and the audience?

    _____

    _____

5. What time of day will I deliver the speech?

    _____

    _____

6. What type of visual aids will be used? How will they be used?

    _____

    _____

Postspeech Analysis Worksheet

Postspeech analysis helps you polish your speaking skills and allows you to learn from your mistakes and successes.

There are **four primary means** to evaluate your speaking skills after the speech.

1.   Nonverbal Responses (e.g., audience applause)

2.   Verbal Responses   (e.g., when an audience member says, "Great speech.")

3.   Survey Responses (e.g., asking audience members questions prepared in a written survey)

4.   Behavioral Responses (e.g., what did your audience do as a result of your speech)

Take a moment to think about your speech and focus on the first two ways of evaluating your speech: Nonverbal and Verbal responses. Write down some notes in the space below based on your observations.

Nonverbal Responses

1.   Did the audience clap at the end of your speech? If so, did it seem sincere?

   _____

2.   Did any of the audience members smile at you at the end of your speech? How did that make you feel?

   _____

3.   Did any of the audience members appear distracted during your speech? For instance, were they reading the newspaper, looking out the window?

   _____

4.   What else did you observe about the audience's nonverbal responses?

   _____

Postspeech Analysis Worksheet

<u>Verbal Responses</u>

1. Were you given any verbal feedback after your speech? If so, what was it?

    _____

    _____

2. Did any audience member comment on your speech topic? If so, what were their comments?

    _____

    _____

3. What comments did you receive from your instructor?

    _____

    _____

BASED ON YOUR **POSTSPEECH ANALYSIS**, RESPOND TO THE FOLLOWING QUESTIONS:

What are your strengths as a speaker?

_____

_____

_____

What do you need to improve upon? And <u>how</u> are you going to do it?

_____

_____

_____

Audience Analysis: Summary Questions

The questions below are designed as learning tools to help you understand how audience analysis affects your speech preparation and delivery.

How does knowing your audience affect your speech delivery?

- _____

- _____

- _____

How does knowing your audience affect your confidence as a speaker?

- _____

- _____

- _____

How does knowing the attitudes of your audience affect your speech preparation and delivery?

- _____

- _____

- _____

How does knowing the speaking environment improve your speech?

- _____

- _____

- _____

Choosing Topics

Choosing a topic for your speech can be the most difficult part of giving a speech. When selecting a topic, you should **keep these three questions in mind:**

- ♦ Who is the audience?

- ♦ What is the occasion?

- ♦ What are my interests, talents, and experiences?

Guidelines for Selecting a Topic

1. **Consider Your Audience**

2. **Consider the Occasion**

3. **Consider Yourself**

Techniques for Selecting a Topic

All successful topics reflect audience, occasion, and speaker. And yet, choosing a topic can be very difficult. Fortunately, there are several techniques that can help you generate speech topics.

Technique #1: **Brainstorming**

Technique #2: **Listening and Reading for Topics**

Technique #3: **Scanning Lists and Indexes**

General Purpose

There are three types of general purposes for giving a speech.

1. **To inform:**   to share information by defining, describing, or explaining.

2. **To persuade:**   to change or reinforce an attitude, belief, value, or behavior.

3. **To entertain:**   to amuse through humor, stories, or other illustrations.

Using Your Experience to Select a Topic

By asking yourself questions, you can generate a long list of potential speech topics. Take a few minutes to answer the questions on this page. Use this page as a brainstorming exercise. Don't critique yourself, just jot down anything that comes to mind.

1. Where have you lived? _____

_____

2. Where have you traveled? What did you find different about these places?

_____

_____

3. What jobs have you had? Explain what you liked about your job and the company.

_____

4. What is your favorite sport? _____

_____

5. What types of television shows do you watch? What issues have they discussed?

_____

_____

6. What were the last books you read? Newspaper articles? _____

_____

7. If you could change two things about the world, what would you change?

_____

_____

Brainstorming Topics

Using the questions you just answered on the previous page, think of the topics you could use for a speech in your class. Take 3-5 minutes and write down every topic that comes to your mind. Don't stop and think about what you are writing, just write!

_____   _____

_____   _____

_____   _____

_____   _____

_____   _____

_____   _____

_____   _____

_____   _____

_____   _____

_____   _____

_____   _____

Now look at your list and pick your 5 favorite topics.

My Five Favorite Topics

1. _____

2. _____

3. _____

4. _____

5. _____

Five Favorite Topics: Worksheet

Transfer your five favorite topics from the previous page.

1. _____

2. _____

3. _____

4. _____

5. _____

	Topic	How I could Narrow	My General Purpose	My Specific Purpose
1.	_____	_____	_____	_____
2.	_____	_____	_____	_____
3.	_____	_____	_____	_____
4.	_____	_____	_____	_____
5.	_____	_____	_____	_____

Audience Analysis as a Topic Guide

A successful speech will be written specifically for a particular audience.
Each speech, therefore, will vary according to your audience.

Using the topics below, think about how your speech would change based on the different audiences given. Write your ideas in the space provided.

Topic: **Recycling**

Audience: **Your Speech Class**   **Environmentalist Group**

_____   _____

_____   _____

_____   _____

_____   _____

Topic: **Sailing**

Audience: **Your Speech Class**   **Senior Citizens Club**

_____   _____

_____   _____

_____   _____

_____   _____

Topic: _____ (write your speech topic here)

Audience: **Your Speech Class**   **Your Parents**

_____   _____

_____   _____

_____   _____

_____   _____

Narrowing Your Purpose

Using the topics below, formulate well-defined specific purposes for the general purpose indicated. **Reminder:** A **specific-purpose sentence** is a concise statement indicating what you want your listeners to be able to do when you finish your speech.

Topic #1:   College

General Purpose: To inform

Specific Purpose: _____

Topic #2:   Law Enforcement

General Purpose: To persuade

Specific Purpose: _____

Topic #3:   Sitcoms of the 1990s

General Purpose: To entertain

My Specific Purpose: _____

Now practice this technique with your own speech topic.

Your Speech Topic: _____

General Purpose: _____

My Specific Purpose: _____

_____

_____

Developing Your Central Idea

Your central idea identifies the essence of your message. Think of it as a one-sentence summary of your speech. An example is provided, and then you can develop the central idea for your speech topic.

Topic: Crime in the United States

General Purpose: To inform.

Specific Purpose: At the end of my speech, the audience will be able to describe the reasons for the increasing crime in the United States.

Central Idea: Violent crime is the most significant problem in society today.

What is your speech topic? Think of at least one option and use it to complete the spaces below.

Topic: _____

General Purpose: _____

Specific Purpose: _____

_____

Central Idea: _____

_____

You will want to go through these steps for each one of your speeches.

Choosing Topics: Summary Questions

The questions below are designed as learning tools to help you understand the importance of choosing speech topics.

What guidelines should you follow when selecting a speech topic?

- ♦ _____
- ♦ _____
- ♦ _____

Why is it important to narrow your speech topic?

- ♦ _____
- ♦ _____
- ♦ _____

What is the difference between a general purpose and a specific purpose?

- ♦ _____
- ♦ _____
- ♦ _____

How does your audience determine the focus of your topic?

- ♦ _____
- ♦ _____
- ♦ _____

Research

Successfully researching for a speech is a difficult task. It requires time, patience, and hard work. The following pages will help you organize your research.

Four Key Research Sources

1. Personal Knowledge and Experience

2. Interviews

    ♦ Open-ended questions
    ♦ Closed-ended questions

3. Mail-order Materials

4. Library Resources

    ♦ Books
    ♦ Periodicals
    ♦ Newspapers
    ♦ Reference materials
    ♦ Government documents

Developing A Research Plan

1. Develop a preliminary bibliography

2. Locate the materials you need

3. Determine which material is most important

4. Take notes as you read

Using Your Four Key Research Sources

Your Speech Topic: _____

With your speech topic in mind, think of how you could use these sources to develop your speech.

1. Personal Knowledge:

    _____

    _____

    _____

    _____

2. Interviews:

    _____

    _____

    _____

    _____

3. Mail-Order Materials:

    _____

    _____

    _____

    _____

4. Library Resources:

    _____

    _____

    _____

    _____

Developing Interview Questions

Interviews can be an excellent means of gaining recent material for your speech. If you are giving a speech on the Japanese education system, you could contact an individual who has gone to school in Japan, or talk with a professor who studies the Japanese culture. Based on the hypothetical interview situation below, develop open-ended and closed-ended questions.

Situation: You are interviewing a doctor on the possibility of universal health coverage.

Open-Ended Questions: Example

1.   How will universal health coverage affect your medical practice?
2.   What do you feel are the benefits of universal health coverage?

My Open-Ended Questions

1. _____

2. _____

Closed-Ended Questions: Example

1. Are you for or against universal health coverage?

My Closed-Ended Question

1.   _____

Now practice this technique with your own speech topic.

Speech Topic: _____

Possible Open-ended Questions:

1. _____

2. _____

Possible Closed-ended Question:

1. _____

Interview Guide

If you are conducting the interview, you are the intervie<u>wer</u>. The person you are interviewing is the interview<u>ee</u>. Use this page as a guide to take with you to interviews.

1. **Name of Interviewee:** _____

2. **Purpose of this interview:** _____
    (write your purpose in the space above, and explain the purpose to the interviewee)

3. **Occupation:** _____

4. **How long have you been in this position/field?:** _____

Write your specific questions here. You may use both closed-and open-ended questions.

♦   _____

    _____

♦   _____

    _____

♦   _____

    _____

♦   _____

    _____

♦   _____

    _____

Current Events Update

A successful speech uses current research and provides timely examples. Being aware of current events will help you think of speech topics, as well as provide excellent and current evidence for your speech.

The questions below will help you think about what's current in the news and how you can use this knowledge in your speech.

Find a local newspaper and scan the front page. What are five headlines on the front page?

1. _____

2. _____

3. _____

4. _____

5. _____

Watch the national news (e.g., CNN) for 20 minutes. What were three major stories the news presented?

1. _____

2. _____

3. _____

Pick up a copy of your school newspaper. What are the current events happening on your campus?

1. _____

2. _____

How can you use this information in your speech?

♦ _____

♦ _____

♦ _____

Research Action Steps

It is important to develop a plan before even stepping foot in the library. This page is designed to help you think and plan before conducting your research.

Your Speech Topic: _____

What is your personal experience with this topic? Think of examples and stories to include in your speech.

_____

_____

Who could you talk to about your speech topic? Think of friends, family, professors, and experts in the field.

_____

_____

What publications will be the most helpful? For example, should you be looking at magazines, newspapers, books, government documents, or all of them? If you are looking for current information, books tend to be more outdated than other publications.

_____

_____

_____

Based on this information, what is the first step you should take to begin your research?

_____

_____

Your Library Hours:

_____

_____

Bibliography Worksheet #1

Your Speech Topic: _____

You will be gathering a lot of material for your speech and it is essential that you keep it well-organized. This worksheet provides one way to organize your sources.

Bibliography Checklist:

1.   Author
2.   Title of book or publication
3.   Title of article, if applicable
4.   Date
5.   Publisher
6.   Page numbers

My Sources:

1.   _____

    _____

2.   _____

    _____

3.   _____

    _____

4.   _____

    _____

5.   _____

    _____

6.   _____

    _____

Bibliography Worksheet #2

Your Speech Topic: _____

You will be gathering a lot of material for your speech and it is essential that you keep it well-organized. This worksheet provides one way to organize your sources.

Bibliography Checklist:

1.   Author
2.   Title of book or publication
3.   Title of article, if applicable
4.   Date
5.   Publisher
6.   Page numbers

My Sources:

1.   _____

    _____

2.   _____

    _____

3.   _____

    _____

4.   _____

    _____

5.   _____

    _____

6.   _____

    _____

Bibliography Worksheet #3

Your Speech Topic: _____

You will be gathering a lot of material for your speech and it is essential that you keep it well-organized. This worksheet provides one way to organize your sources.

<u>Bibliography Checklist</u>:

1. Author
2. Title of book or publication
3. Title of article, if applicable
4. Date
5. Publisher
6. Page numbers

<u>My Sources</u>:

1. _____

_____

2. _____

_____

3. _____

_____

4. _____

_____

5. _____

_____

6. _____

_____

Research: Summary Questions

These questions are designed as learning tools to assist you in your research efforts.

Why is it important to have an interview guide when you go to an interview?

- ◆ _____

- ◆ _____

- ◆ _____

How can you keep yourself updated on current events?

- ◆ _____

- ◆ _____

- ◆ _____

Why is it important to develop a research plan before going to the library?

- ◆ _____

- ◆ _____

- ◆ _____

What are the components you should include in your bibliography?

- ◆ _____

- ◆ _____

- ◆ _____

Supporting Your Speech

Supporting materials not only help a speaker capture and maintain an audience's attention, but they also serve as evidence to support what the speaker says. Without relevant examples and solid statistics, a speaker's ideas may be dismissed as hot air.

Types of Supporting Material

1. Examples and Illustrations
   - brief examples
   - extended illustrations
   - hypothetical illustrations

2. Explanations and Descriptions

3. Definitions

4. Analogies
   - literal
   - figurative

5. Statistics

6. Opinions or Expert Testimony
   - testimonies of expert authorities
   - quotations from literary works

Criteria for Selecting the Best Supporting Materials

1. Proximity

2. Significance

3. Concreteness

4. Variety

5. Humor

6. Suitability

Identifying Supporting Materials

The following statements represent various types of supporting material. Read each statement and then identify the type of supporting material it contains. If it contains more than one type, identify all the types present.

1.   Last year we served 208 more patients than the previous year. That's an increase of 4.4 percent.

      Type of Support: _____

2.   Sal Thomas, a leading scholar from Northwestern University, has studied the effects and detriments of cholesterol for 15 years now. His research indicates that the harmful effects of cholesterol build-up cannot be reversed with a regular exercise plan and major change in diet.

      Type of Support: _____

3.   My topic today is long-term training plans. When I speak of "long-term," I'm referring to 10 years down the road.

      Type of Support: _____

4.   Coronary heart disease is the nation's number one killer. Six million Americans currently suffer from it.

      Type of Support: _____

5.   School is like a track meet. To be successful, you must clearly negotiate all the hurdles.

      Type of Support: _____

Supporting Materials for Your Speech

Use this page to begin gathering supporting material for your speech. A good speech will utilize several different types of supporting material. Be sure to include your source after each type of supporting material.

Topic for Speech #1: _____

A. *Example or illustration* _____

_____

_____

B. *Explanation or description* _____

_____

_____

C. *Definition* _____

_____

D. *Analogy* _____

_____

_____

E. *Statistics* _____

_____

_____

F. *Opinion or expert testimony* _____

_____

_____

Supporting Materials for Your Speech

Use this page to begin gathering supporting material for your speech. A good speech will utilize several different types of supporting material.

Topic for Speech #2: _____

A. *Example or illustration* _____

_____

_____

B. *Explanation or description* _____

_____

_____

C. *Definition* _____

_____

D. *Analogy* _____

_____

_____

E. *Statistics* _____

_____

_____

F. *Opinion or expert testimony* _____

_____

_____

Supporting Materials for Your Speech

Use this page to begin gathering supporting material for your speech. A good speech will utilize several different types of supporting material.

Topic for Speech #3: _____

A. *Example or illustration* _____

_____

_____

B. *Explanation or description* _____

_____

_____

C. *Definition* _____

_____

D. *Analogy* _____

_____

_____

E. *Statistics* _____

_____

_____

F. *Opinion or expert testimony* _____

_____

_____

Selecting Supporting Material

Read the statements below. Take a stance on each statement, that is, do you agree or disagree? After each statement, write in the kinds of supporting materials you would likely use to support your position.

1.   The fear of giving a speech can be reduced.

_____

_____

2.   Second-hand smoke is harmful.

_____

_____

3.   Student fees should not be raised.

_____

_____

What kinds of supporting material would likely support your speech topics?

Topic #1: _____

_____

Topic #2: _____

_____

Topic #3: _____

_____

Supporting Material Checklist

1. Examples and Illustrations

    ___ Are they clearly explained?
    ___ Are they relevant to your main point?
    ___ Are they representative?
    ___ Can the audience relate to them?

2. Explanations and Descriptions

    ___ Are they brief?
    ___ Are they specific and concrete?

3. Definitions

    ___ Are your definitions clear and understandable?
    ___ Are the definitions necessary?
    ___ Are the definitions common and not controversial?

4. Analogies

    ___ Have you made the similarities clear?
    ___ Do they increase the audience's ability to understand the issues?

5. Statistics

    ___ Did you round off numbers whenever possible?
    ___ Are your sources reliable?
    ___ Are they accurate?

6. Opinions or Expert Testimony

    ___ Are the people you cited experts in the area?
    ___ Have you identified the qualifications of the experts?

Supporting Your Speech: Summary Questions

The questions below are designed to help you understand the use of supporting material in your speech.

What are the different types of supporting material available for your speech?

- ♦ _____
- ♦ _____
- ♦ _____

Why is it important to include several different types of supporting material in your speech?

- ♦ _____
- ♦ _____
- ♦ _____

What do you think is the strongest type of supporting material? Why?

- ♦ _____
- ♦ _____
- ♦ _____

Organizing Your Speech

Organizational Patterns

1. Chronological

2. Topical

3. Spatial

4. Causal

5. Problem-solution

Arranging your Supporting Materials

1. Primacy or Recency

2. Specificity

3. Complexity

4. "Soft" to "Hard" Evidence

Integrating Supporting Materials Into Your Speech

1. State the main idea.

2. Cite the source of the supporting material.

3. Present the supporting material.

4. Restate the main idea.

Types of Signposts

1. Transitions

2. Previews

3. Summaries

Organizational Patterns

For each central idea below, choose the organizational pattern that would <u>best</u> fit the given central idea.

1. A speech describing how to make sushi.

   _____

2. A speech describing IBM's plan to decrease the number of sexual harassment claims.

   _____

3. A speech explaining the greatest mountain ranges in Switzerland.

   _____

4. A speech describing the reasons for increasing gang violence.

   _____

5. A speech explaining the development of the personal computer.

   _____

6. A speech discussing airline safety in Canada, the United States, and Mexico.

   _____

Using Organizational Patterns

The following example illustrates how speech topics may follow many organizational patterns.

Sample Speech Topic: Drug Testing

Chronological (past, present, future or a how-to speech)

1. Early attempts for drug testing in the United States military

2. Drug testing and the workplace today

3. The future of drug testing in American society

Topical (natural or logical divisions)

1. The reasons for drug testing

2. The effectiveness of drug testing

3. Drug testing and the Constitution: Is it constitutional?

Spatial (arranged according to location or direction)

1. Drug testing in the military

2. Drug testing of federal government employees

3. Drug testing of private sector employees

Causal (shows a cause and effect)

1. Successful drug testing programs in corporate America

2. Declining workplace accidents

Problem-Solution (shows a problem and the best way to solve it)

1. Harms of drug use in the workplace

2. Employee-sponsored drug testing programs

Using Organizational Patterns

Given your speech topic, how do you determine which organizational pattern to use? The best way to determine this is to plan out your speech using several different formats, and then to choose the best one.

Your Speech Topic: _____

Use the space below to see how your main points might fit into the different organizational patterns.

Chronological (past, present, future or a how-to speech)

1. _____

2. _____

3. _____

Topical (natural or logical divisions)

1. _____

2. _____

3. _____

Spatial (arranged according to location, direction, or geography)

1. _____

2. _____

3. _____

Causal (shows a cause and effect)

1. _____

2. _____

Using Organizational Patterns

Your Speech Topic: _____

Problem-Solution (shows a problem and the best way to solve it)

1. _____

2. _____

What pattern provides the best audience-centered speech? Review all of your ideas above and choose the one which allows you to write and deliver a successful, audience-centered speech.

The best organizational pattern for my topic: _____

Why is this the best organizational pattern? Explain your reasons for choosing this particular pattern.

_____

_____

_____

_____

Arranging Your Supporting Materials

You have now decided what supporting materials to use and where they should go in your speech. But suppose you have an illustration, two statistics, and an opinion to support your second main point. What order do you put these in?

Four internal organizational strategies are commonly used to decide how to place your evidence within each main point.

Strategy #1: Primacy or Recency

♦ The **principle of primacy** suggests that you put the most important idea **first**. If your topic is extremely controversial and your audience is likely to be neutral or hostile, you should present your most powerful supporting material first.

♦ According to the **principle of recency**, the event discussed **last** is usually the one the audience will remember best. Speakers often save the "clincher" for last, so the audience will remember it.

Strategy #2: Specificity

♦ Sometimes your supporting materials will range from very specific examples to more general overviews of a situation. You may either offer your specific information first and end with your general statement or make the general statement first and support it with specific evidence.

Strategy #3: Complexity

♦ In many situations, it makes sense to start with the simplest ideas that are easy to understand and work up to more complex ones.

Strategy #4: "Soft" to "Hard" Evidence

♦ Soft supporting materials are based mainly on opinion or inference. Hypothetical illustrations, definitions, analogies, and opinions are usually considered soft.

♦ Hard evidence includes factual examples and statistics. Soft-to-hard organization of supporting materials relies chiefly on the idea that the last statement will be remembered best.

Arranging Your Supporting Materials

The following three pieces of supporting material are a fictitious example.

Code	Supporting Material
A:	Carol Martin studied the national health care system in Canada while in school. She interviewed a total of 10 health care providers and patients. Her conclusion: that the United States must implement a universal health coverage.
B:	Dan is a small business owner. He has worked hard for many years to build a successful business. He thinks national health care is a bad idea.
C:	A 1993 Smith/Klein survey reported that 1 in 2 Americans believe that national health care is a step in the right direction. This means that half of the people in this classroom are in favor of some national health care.

Each piece of supporting material has been coded with a letter (i.e., "A," "B," and "C"). Your goal is to re-arrange this material according to the different internal organizational patterns. Rather than writing the entire piece of supporting material, use the codes provided.

Arrange the three pieces of supporting material above so they represent:

#1: Primacy Strategy:

_____ Most Powerful   _____ Least Powerful   _____ Clincher

#2: Specificity Strategy:

_____ Most General   _____ More Specific   _____ Most Specific

#3: Complexity Strategy:

_____ Simple   _____ More Complex   _____ Most Complex

#4: "Soft" to "Hard" Strategy:

_____ Soft   _____ Harder   _____ Hardest

Using Transitions

Now that you have chosen the most effective organizational pattern for your speech, let's focus on writing your transitions to ensure a well-organized speech.

Write your main points in the spaces provided. After each main point, develop a transition between your main points. Remember, a transition acts as a bridge between your ideas.

Main Point #1: _____

Transition between Main Point 1 & 2: _____

_____

_____

Main Point #2: _____

Transition between Main Point 2 & 3: _____

_____

_____

Main Point #3: _____

Transition between Main Point 3 and Conclusion: _____

_____

_____

Organizing Your Speech: Summary Questions

These questions are designed to help you think about the importance of organizing your speech.

Why is it important to have a clear organizational format for your speech?

- ◆ _____

- ◆ _____

- ◆ _____

How can you use different organizational strategies to make your speech more audience-centered?

- ◆ _____

- ◆ _____

- ◆ _____

Why is it important to use transitions in your speech?

- ◆ _____

- ◆ _____

- ◆ _____

Outlining

Outlines are an effective tool for organizing your ideas. Well-presented speeches are most often the result of a complete outline.

Types of Outlines

1. Preparation Outline: includes all main ideas, subpoints, and supporting materials to be used in the main portion, or body, of a speech. It also includes the specific purpose, central idea, introduction, conclusion, and transitions.

2. Audience Outline: single words and phrases are most common. It is not as detailed as the preparation outline. It is rarely written in complete sentences.

3. Delivery Outline: includes only the information you will need to present your speech in the fashion you have planned and rehearsed. A delivery outline should not be so detailed that you find yourself reading it rather than speaking to your audience.

Developing a Preparation Outline: Guidelines

You will most likely be asked to develop a preparation outline for each of your classroom speeches. The guidelines below will help you develop an effective preparation outline.

1. **Write your preparation outline in complete sentences.**

2. **Use correct outline form.**

    a. **Use standard outline numbering.** Based on the principle of subordination, it follows this sequence:
        I. First main point
           A. First subpoint of I
           B. Second subpoint of I
              1. First subpoint of B
              2. Second subpoint of B
                 a. First subpoint of 2
                 b. Second subpoint of 2
        II. Second main point

    b. **Each subpoint has at least two subdivisions, if it has any.**

        Remember, every capital A must have a B, every 1 must have a 2.

    c. **Points, subpoints, and supporting material must be properly indented.**
        Main points, indicated by Roman numerals, are written closest to the left margin.

        I.   First main point
        II.   Second main point
        III.   Third main point

        Subpoint A begins directly underneath the first <u>word</u> of point I:

        I. Every speech has three parts.
           A. The first part is the introduction.
           B. The second part is the body.
           C. The third part is the conclusion.

    d. **The first word of each point at each level is capitalized.**

    e. **All points at the same level are parallel in structure.**

3. **Write and label your purpose statement and central idea at the top of your preparation outline.**

4. **After you have decided on key transitions, previews, summaries, introduction, and conclusion, add these to your outline.**

Practice Developing an Outline

This exercise gives you an opportunity to practice the guidelines presented on the previous page. Each of the sentences below are elements, that when put together, make up an outline on South Africa. The format of the outline is given to you below. Put the number of each sentence in the correct spot on the outline.

1. Terrorist bombs and assassinations occurred prior to the elections.

2. Rebuilding a free South Africa will be long and difficult.

3. The National Party led by De Klerk lost the Presidency.

4. Prior to the election, tremendous violence had disrupted the country.

5. Nelson Mandela of the ANC is the first black President of South Africa.

6. Most roads were built to purposely avoid non-white, rural areas.

7. 14,000 black South Africans were killed between 1989 & 1994.

8. South Africa held its first free election in 1994.

9. The infrastructure was neglected throughout the countryside.

10. Many South Africans outside the cities do not have running water.

11. The first popularly elected President took control in May of 1994.

12. Future unrest will likely be economic in nature, not political.

I. _____

   A. _____
      1. _____
      2. _____

   B. _____
      1. _____
      2. _____

   C. _____
      1. _____
        a. _____
        b. _____
      2. _____

Practice Critiquing an Outline

The following is a <u>preparation outline</u>. This outline details a speech on Major League Baseball realignment. This outline contains a number of errors in form. Find as many flaws in the outline as you can.

Speech Topic: Baseball Realignment

Purpose Statement: At the end of my speech the audience will be able to discuss major league baseball realignment.

A. Major league owners voted to divide each of the two leagues into three geographic divisions.

   1. at one time the current divisions made sense, but as the league expanded over the years, teams were placed regardless of geography.

      a. Owners voted 27 to 1 in favor of realignment.

      b. A survey showed that fans support the change.

B. The player's union said that the new alignment would be beneficial for baseball.

   1. The player's association actually introduced the format that the owners approved.

      a. post season play will consist of eight teams rather than four.

      b. teams grouped geographically.

Some of the problems you may have found are:

1. This outline does not contain a central idea, introduction, or conclusion.

2. No transitions are presented.

3. The first words of each point is not capitalized.

4. Each subpoint does not have at least two divisions (if 1, must be a 2).

5. All points are not in complete sentences.

6. All subdivisions must relate to the original points.

Writing Your Preparation Outline

The following pages include a blank preparation outline for you to begin organizing your speech ideas. This serves only as a starting point. Blank space has been left below each main point so that you may add your subpoints and supporting material in any format you choose (as long as you use the correct outline form described on the previous page).

Speech Topic: _____

Purpose: _____

Central Idea: _____

Introduction: _____

_____

_____

_____

_____

I. *First Main Point* _____

_____

_____

_____

_____

_____

_____

_____

_____

Transition: _____

Writing Your Preparation Outline (continued)

II. *Second Main Point* _____

_____

_____

_____

_____

_____

Transition: _____

III. *Third Main Point* _____

_____

_____

_____

_____

_____

Transition: _____

Conclusion: _____

_____

_____

_____

_____

Writing Your Audience Outline

The blank audience outline below is designed for you to shorten and simplify your complete preparation outline. This serves as a roadmap for your speech. Blank space has been left below each main point so that you may add your subpoints. This format should stem from your preparation outline you just completed.

Purpose: _____

Central Idea: _____

Introduction: _____

_____

Preview Statement: _____

_____

_____

I. _____
   A. _____
   B. _____
   C. _____

II. _____
   A. _____
   B. _____
   C. _____

III. _____
   A. _____
   B. _____
   C. _____

Conclusion: _____

_____

_____

Utilizing the Delivery Outline

Your delivery outline becomes the actual notes that you speak from as you perform your speech. To be successful, this outline needs to be transferred to note cards. Note cards are better than regular paper as they are easier to handle comfortably. Paper also has a tendency to rustle, and, as a consequence, may distract your audience.

Follow these suggestions for successfully writing and using your delivery outline.

1. Two or three 4-by-6 inch or 5-by-8 inch note cards will give you enough space for a delivery outline; the number of cards you use depends on the length of your speech. These cards are small enough to hold in one hand, and stiff enough not to rustle.

2. Type or print your delivery outline neatly on <u>one</u> side of the note cards.

3. Make sure that the letters and words on the cards are large enough so that you can see them easily.

4. Include citations for expert testimonies and statistics on note cards.

5. Number the note cards. This will prevent fiascos resulting from out-of-order notes.

6. Add delivery cues and reminders, such as "Slow Down," "Pause," or simply "Relax" on your note cards.

7. Highlight material you have difficulty recalling.

8. If you don't need your note cards, don't use them.

9. Do not read directly from your note cards; only glance at them while keeping audience eye contact.

10. Practice giving your speech while standing and using your note cards.

Outlining: Summary Questions

The questions below are designed to increase your understanding of the uses and benefits of outlines when preparing a speech.

Why is it necessary to write a detailed outline before giving a speech?

- _____

- _____

- _____

What, in your opinion, are the most important guidelines for preparing note cards?

- _____

- _____

- _____

Why is a delivery outline constructed?

- _____

- _____

- _____

Introducing and Concluding Your Speech

The introduction and conclusion of a message are vital to achieving your communication goals. While making up only 20 percent of the total speech, the introduction and conclusion provide audiences with important first and final impressions of the speaker and the speech.

Five Purposes of the Introduction

1.   Gain the audience's attention

2.   Introduce the subject

3.   Give the audience a reason to listen

4.   Establish your credibility

5.   Preview your main ideas

Ten ways to Introduce a Speech

1.   Illustrations
2.   Startling fact or statistics
3.   Quotations
4.   Humor
5.   Questions
6.   References to a historical event
7.   References to recent events
8.   Personal references
9.   References to the occasion
10. References to preceding speeches

Four Purposes of the Conclusion

1.   Summarize the speech

2.   Reemphasize the main idea in a memorable way

3.   Motivate the audience to respond

4.   Provide closure

Write Your Introduction

Speech Topic #1: _____

One of the key purposes of your introduction is to provide an overview of your message. Use this page as a draft for the introduction of your first speech.

Attention Getter: _____

_____

_____

_____

Introduce Your Subject: _____

_____

_____

_____

Reason to Listen: _____

_____

_____

_____

Credibility: _____

_____

_____

_____

Preview: _____

_____

_____

Write Your Introduction

Speech Topic #2: _____

One of the key purposes of your introduction is to provide an overview of your message. Use this page as a draft for the introduction of your second speech.

Attention Getter: _____

_____

_____

_____

Introduce Your Subject: _____

_____

_____

_____

Reason to Listen: _____

_____

_____

_____

Credibility: _____

_____

_____

_____

Preview: _____

_____

_____

Write Your Introduction

Speech Topic #3: _____

One of the key purposes of your introduction is to provide an overview of your message. Use this page as a draft for the introduction of your third speech.

Attention Getter: _____

_____

_____

_____

Introduce Your Subject: _____

_____

_____

_____

Reason to Listen: _____

_____

_____

_____

Credibility: _____

_____

_____

_____

Preview: _____

_____

_____

Creating Attention Getters

The first words of your speech need to create a strong first impression that grabs the attention of your audience. There are many creative ways to capture their attention. Use your creativity to write down a few options and then practice them on a friend. This will help to ensure that you choose the best attention getter.

1.   **Illustration** _____

_____

2.   **Startling fact or statistic** _____

_____

3.   **Quotation** _____

_____

4.   **Humor** _____

_____

5.   **Question** _____

_____

6.   **Reference to a historical event** _____

_____

7.   **Reference to recent events** _____

_____

8.   **Personal reference** _____

_____

9.   **Reference to the occasion** _____

_____

10. **Reference to preceding speeches** _____

_____

WHICH OPTION WORKED BEST? _____

Introduction Tips and Checklist

Use this page to evaluate your speech introductions. Make some notes in the spaces provided.

♦ How did you begin your speech? _____

♦ Did you avoid beginning a speech with the formula, "This evening, I'd like you to consider. . " or "The topic of my speech is . . ." _____

♦ Did the class react favorably to the beginning of your speech? _____

♦ How long was your introduction? Is it too lengthy? _____

♦ Did you use descriptive illustrations, examples, and statistics? _____

♦ Were you specific with people, places, and events? _____

♦ Review your introduction once again and be sure you have fulfilled all 5 purposes of the speech introduction.

_____   Attention Getter

_____   Introduce Subject

_____   Reason to Listen

_____   Credibility

_____   Preview of Main Points

♦ Which of the five parts of the introduction were you most happy with? _____

♦ Which of the five parts do you need to improve in your next speech? _____

Write Your Conclusion

Your conclusion leaves an important final impression. Long after you finish speaking, your audience is likely to remember the effect, if not the content, of your closing remarks.
Use this page as a draft for the conclusion of your first speech.

Speech Topic #1: _____

Summarize: _____

_____

_____

_____

Reemphasize in memorable way: _____

_____

_____

_____

Motivate Audience: _____

_____

_____

_____

Provide Closure: _____

_____

_____

_____

Write Your Conclusion

Your conclusion leaves an important final impression. Long after you finish speaking, your audience is likely to remember the effect, if not the content, of your closing remarks.
Use this page as a draft for the conclusion of your second speech.

Speech Topic #2: _____

Summarize: _____

_____

_____

_____

Reemphasize in memorable way: _____

_____

_____

_____

Motivate Audience: _____

_____

_____

_____

Provide Closure: _____

_____

_____

_____

Write Your Conclusion

Your conclusion leaves an important final impression. Long after you finish speaking, your audience is likely to remember the effect, if not the content, of your closing remarks. Use this page as a draft for the conclusion of your third speech.

Speech Topic #3: _____

Summarize: _____

_____

_____

_____

Reemphasize in memorable way: _____

_____

_____

_____

Motivate Audience: _____

_____

_____

_____

Provide Closure: _____

_____

_____

_____

Conclusion Tips and Checklist

Use this page to evaluate your conclusions. Make some notes in the spaces provided.

- Did your conclusion restate your main idea in a memorable way? If so, how? Did you rely on a famous quotation? _____

  _____

- Does your conclusion include the use of emotion? _____

- Did you use some sort of nonverbal or verbal closure to end your speech? _____

- Did the audience know you were finished when you completed the speech? _____

- Now look at your introduction AND conclusion. Did you make a reference to your introduction in your conclusion? _____

- Review your conclusion once again and be sure you have fulfilled all 4 purposes of the speech conclusion.

  _____   Summarize the Speech

  _____   Reemphasize the Main Idea

  _____   Motivate the Audience to Respond

  _____   Provide Closure

- Which of the four parts of the conclusion did you cover the best? _____

- Which of the four parts do you need to improve in your next speech? _____

Introducing & Concluding Your Speech:
Summary Questions

These questions are designed to increase your understanding and summarize what you learned about introducing and concluding your speech.

Why is it important to give the audience a reason to listen?

♦ _____

♦ _____

♦ _____

How can you establish your credibility in a speech?

♦ _____

♦ _____

♦ _____

What is the benefit of using a preview statement in your introduction?

♦ _____

♦ _____

♦ _____

How can you motivate your audience to respond?

♦ _____

♦ _____

♦ _____

Types of Speeches

Types of Informative Speeches

1. Speeches about Ideas

2. Speeches about Objects

3. Speeches about Procedures

4. Speeches about People

5. Speeches about Events

Key Methods of Informing

1. Defining

2. Describing

3. Narrating

Persuasive Speeches

1. Problem-solution

2. Refutation

3. Cause and effect

4. Motivated Sequence

Seven Types of Ceremonial Speeches

1. Introductions

2. Award Presentations and Nominations

3. Acceptances

4. Commencement Addresses

5. Commemorative Addresses

6. Eulogies

7. Keynote Addresses

Informative Speaking

To inform is to teach someone something you know. You have probably heard more informative speeches than any other type of speech. There are many different types of informative speeches. The goal is to choose an audience-centered topic that you enjoy learning and speaking about.

Your Informative Speech Topic: _____

Think about your informative topic. What type of informative speech is it?

_____

♦ Is it a speech about ideas? ____

Speeches about ideas are usually more abstract than the other types of speeches. Principles, concepts, and theories are at the heart of idea speeches. Most speeches about ideas are organized topically or according to complexity.

♦ Is it a speech about objects? ____

A speech about an object might be about anything tangible--anything you can see or touch. You may choose to show the actual object to your audience while you are talking about it. Speeches about objects may be organized topically or chronologically. If a how-to discussion becomes the central focus of a speech, it then becomes a speech about procedure.

♦ Is it a speech about procedures? ____

A speech about a procedure discusses how something works or describes a process that produces a particular outcome. At the close of such a speech, your audience should be able to describe, understand, or perform the procedure you have described. Most speeches about a procedure consist of a chronological progression.

♦ Is it a speech about people? ____

A biographical speech could be about someone famous or about someone you know personally. These speeches should give your listeners the feeling that the person is a unique, authentic individual. These speeches may be organized chronologically, as well as topically.

♦ Is it a speech about events? ____

Major events punctuate our lives and mark the passage of time. A major event can form the basis of a fascinating informative speech. You can choose to talk about an event that you have either witnessed or researched. Most speeches about events follow a chronological arrangement, but may also be organized topically.

Practice Writing a Story

Everyone likes to hear a story. The anecdote or illustration helps your listeners visualize what they hear. When telling your story, make it interesting by paying careful attention to details and descriptions.

When you tell stories in a speech, you are using the **narrating** method of informing your audience. Telling an effective story takes a lot of thought and practice.

Most good stories follow a four-part structure:

1. **Opening:** Set the stage for the action you are about to describe. You need to appeal to your audience's senses and draw a mental picture for them.

2. **Complication:** Describe some difficulty, conflict, or problem to arouse interest and develop the drama.

3. **Climax:** Develop the complication to a climax.

4. **Resolution:** Finish the story and tie up the loose ends to provide a satisfying ending.

Now practice writing a story for your speech. What story could you tell with your topic?

Opening _____

_____

Complication _____

_____

Climax _____

_____

Resolution _____

_____

Did you link your story to your main idea? Practice delivering your story several times!

71   (c) 1994 by Prentice-Hall, Inc.

Persuasive Speaking

Persuasion can be defined as the process of changing or reinforcing attitudes, beliefs, values, or behavior.

There are several special ways to organize persuasive speeches. Specific approaches to organizing speeches depend on audience, message, and desired objective.

The next few pages explain **four** organizational patterns and provide examples for each pattern.

Organizational Strategy: Problem-Solution

The most basic organizational pattern for a persuasive speech is to make the audience aware of the problem, then present a solution that clearly solves it.

The problem-solution pattern works best when a clearly evident problem can be documented and a solution can be proposed to deal with the evils of the well-documented problem.

EXAMPLE:

Problem: Our company has experienced a dramatic increase of sexual harassment claims in the past six months.

Solution: Design and deliver a training program to increase sensitivity on sexuality issues. The training program will also include suggestions for creating an organization policy on sexual harassment.

Now see how your topic might fit into this pattern.

Your Persuasive Speech Topic: _____

Problem: _____

_____

_____

Solution: _____

_____

_____

Persuasive Speaking

Organizational Strategy: Refutation

This strategy seeks to prove that the arguments against your position are false. To use refutation as a strategy for persuasion, you first identify objections to your position that your listeners may hold and then refute or overcome those objections with arguments and evidence.

EXAMPLE:

Objections to Your Position: Some of you may believe that crime is increasing dramatically.

Refutation: The most recent study on crime suggests that not all types of crimes are increasing, and that overall, the number of criminal acts per 100,000 people is decreasing in the United States.

Now see how your topic might fit into this pattern.

Your Persuasive Speech Topic: _____

Objections to Your Position: _____

_____

_____

_____

Refutation: _____

_____

_____

_____

How does this persuasive strategy change the focus of your speech? Compare it to the problem-solution strategy and see which one is the best for your audience.

(c) 1994 by Prentice-Hall, Inc.

Persuasive Speaking

Organizational Strategy: Cause and Effect

1. You could also organize a message by noting the cause and then spelling out the effects the cause has.

2. One way to use the cause-effect method is to begin with an effect or problem and then identify the causes of the problem in an effort to convince your listeners that the problem is significant.

EXAMPLES:

Form #1:

Cause: Millions of Americans are exposed to tobacco smoke daily.

Effect: Thousands of Americans die each year of lung cancer from tobacco smoke.

Form #2:

Effect or Problem: 100,00 teenagers start smoking each year.

Cause: Tobacco companies appear to be targeting teenagers with their advertisements.

Now see how your topic might fit into this pattern.

Your Persuasive Speech Topic: _____

Cause: _____

_____

_____

Effect: _____

_____

_____

How does this strategy change your approach?

Persuasive Speaking: The Motivated Sequence

The motivated sequence is a five-step organizational plan that has proved successful for several decades. It is one of the most commonly used outlines for persuasive speeches. Each step is described below. After reviewing the steps, you will have a chance to fill in the Motivated Sequence for your persuasive outline.

Five Steps of the Motivated Sequence

1. **Attention:** Your first goal is to get your listener's attention. The ten methods of gaining your audience's attention were discussed in the previous chapter.

2. **Need:** Establish why your topic, problem, or issue should concern listeners. Tell your listeners why there is a need for change. You must also convince your listeners that this need for a change affects them directly.

3. **Satisfaction:** Identify how your plan will satisfy the need. What is your solution to the problem? At this point, you need not go in great detail.

4. **Visualization:** You need to give your audience a sense of what it would be like if your solution were or were not adopted.

5. **Action:** This last step forms the basis of your conclusion. You tell your audience the specific action they can take to implement your solution. Identify exactly what you want your listeners to do. Give them simple, clear, easy-to-follow steps to achieve your goal.

Use the next page to begin writing a persuasive outline using the Motivated Sequence.

The Motivated Sequence
Persuasive Outline

Persuasive Speech Topic: _____

I.   **Attention Step** _____

_____

_____

II. **Need Step** _____

_____

_____

_____

III. **Satisfaction Step** _____

_____

_____

_____

IV. **Visualization Step** _____

_____

_____

_____

V.   **Action Step** _____

_____

_____

_____

Impromptu Speaking

Most of us have been called on at one time or another to deliver a spur-of-the-moment or impromptu speech.

Impromptu delivery occurs when a speaker has only a very brief period in which to gather thoughts and then present them to an audience. Preparation time is practically nonexistent, ranging from a few seconds to a few minutes.

These guidelines can help ease you through an impromptu speech:

1. Consider your audience.

2. Be brief.

3. Speak honestly, but with reserve, from personal experience and knowledge.

4. Organize! Effective impromptu speakers will organize their ideas into an introduction, body, and conclusion.

Now practice developing a delivery outline for some sample topics:

> Topic #1: Problems in higher education
>
> Topic #2: What are my career goals?
>
> Topic #3: Freedom

Introduction: _____

_____

Body:

    Main Point #1: _____

    Main Point #2: _____

    Main point #3: _____

Conclusion: _____

_____

Types of Speeches: Summary Questions

These questions are designed to help you understand the different types of speeches that you may be asked to deliver.

Why is selecting the proper type of informative speech important?

◆ _____

◆ _____

◆ _____

How do you select the best persuasive organizational pattern for your speech?

◆ _____

◆ _____

◆ _____

Why does the inclusion of good stories help your speech?

◆ _____

◆ _____

◆ _____

What are the key elements of a good impromptu speech?

◆ _____

◆ _____

◆ _____

Writing Your Speech

CONGRATULATIONS!! You have made it through several chapters and are now ready to write your speech.

Remember, the introduction of your speech is most often written last. So you might begin by writing your main ideas. Begin this process by brainstorming a list of potential areas within your topic that you may want to cover.

Speech Topic: _____

Potential Main Ideas (topic areas):

- ♦ _____
- ♦ _____
- ♦ _____
- ♦ _____
- ♦ _____
- ♦ _____
- ♦ _____
- ♦ _____

From the list that you have generated, choose three topic areas that fit well together. You may want to combine or subdivide areas from the list above. The goal is to make sure that you feel comfortable speaking on these areas. These topic areas then become your three main points.

Main Idea #1: _____
_____
_____

Main Idea #2: _____
_____
_____

Main Idea #3: _____
_____
_____

Writing Speech Tips and Reminders

Tip #1:

If you have written in your main points, review them once again. What organizational pattern are you using? Is it the most effective pattern for your particular topic?

Tip #2:

Review your main points. What types of supporting material are you using? Are you using a variety of sources? Or are you loading up your speech with one particular type of supporting material?

Remember you have six types of supporting material to choose from:

Examples and Illustrations
Explanations and Descriptions
Definitions
Analogies
Statistics
Opinions

Tip #3:

Have you written your conclusion yet? If so, have you fulfilled the four purposes of your speech conclusion?

Tip #4:

Refer back to your conclusion now. How have you made your speech conclusion memorable? If you can't describe it, you probably haven't made it especially memorable. Remember, "end with a bang" so your audience remembers your speech.

Tip #5:

Have you written your introduction yet? If so, review it and double check that you have fulfilled all five purposes of the speech introduction.

Tip #6:

Review your introduction. Are the first sentences in your introduction designed to capture the audience's attention? What method or methods have you used to gain the audience's attention?

Speech Outline Checklist

This checklist is provided as a tool to use as you near the end of writing your speech outline. Review each of the items and check them against your outline.

Introduction: Have you fulfilled all 5 purposes?

_____ Attention Getter
_____ Introduce Subject
_____ Reason to Listen
_____ Credibility
_____ Preview of Main Points

Transitions: Do they connect the main points together?

Evidence: Are the sources clear?

_____ Every piece of evidence has a citation
_____ Every citation can be clearly traced to the bibliography
_____ The bibliography contains every source cited in the outline

Conclusion: Have you fulfilled all 4 purposes?

_____ Summarize the Speech
_____ Reemphasize the Main Idea
_____ Motivate the Audience to Respond
_____ Provide Closure

Outlining: Have you neatly outlined your information?

_____ Complete sentences
_____ Use standard outline numbering
_____ Each subpoint has at least two subdivisions, if it has any
_____ Properly indented
_____ Capitalization of first word of each point
_____ All points at the same level are parallel in structure

Delivery Tips & Guidelines

A. **Attitude and Preparation:**
    1. Be confident. You're as good as anyone else!

    2. Be positive about your topic, the audience, and yourself.

    3. Be assertive. Tell people what you want to tell them. Don't be wishy-washy: "I was wondering if we could kinda discuss something that is sorta important..."

    4. Practice, Practice, Practice!!! It will be apparent if you don't.

    5. Think of your speech as an expanded conversation. No one wants to hear a "canned speech"--BE COMMUNICATIVE.

B. **Hand Gestures:**
    1. Your hands are an important tool to add enthusiasm to your delivery.

    2. They should be used to make a point. Don't glue them to the podium or keep your hands at the sides of your body all the time.

    4. Gestures should be relaxed, not stiff and choppy.

    5. Avoid preening gestures (straightening hair, ties, skirt, etc).

C. **Eye Contact:**
    1. Your most immediate form of nonverbal feedback.

    2. Try not to look only at one person. Share your eye contact with the entire audience.

D. **Volume:**
    1. Know what volume your voice should be in your classroom.

    2. Speaking loudly and/or whispering may be an effective way to make a particular point.

E. **Enunciation:**
    1. Speak with your mouth open to make your words sound clear--don't mumble.

    2. Practice any words you have difficulty pronouncing.

F. **Overall:**
    1. Picture yourself giving a great speech--your attitude is half the battle!

    2. Please do not apologize for anything. We will know if you have a cold or such, there is no need to tell us.

    3. GOOD LUCK!

Self-Analysis

Speech Topic: _____

It is always a good idea to evaluate yourself after you speak. Answer these questions <u>after</u> you have delivered your speech in class. Going through this self-analysis will help to build your confidence and competence as a speaker.

How did your preparation affect your speech performance? Could you have been more prepared? _____

_____

_____

I think that my greatest strength during this speech was: _____

_____

_____

The one speaking skill that I can most improve upon is: _____

_____

_____

How can you continue to improve as a speaker? _____

_____

_____

How did the audience respond to you and your speech? _____

_____

_____

Write any other comments you may have here: _____

_____

Self-Analysis

Speech Topic: _____

It is always a good idea to evaluate yourself after you speak. Answer these questions <u>after</u> you have delivered your speech in class. Going through this self-analysis will help to build your confidence and competence as a speaker.

How did your preparation affect your speech performance? Could you have been more prepared? _____

_____

_____

I think that my greatest strength during this speech was: _____

_____

_____

The one speaking skill that I can most improve upon is: _____

_____

_____

How can you continue to improve as a speaker? _____

_____

_____

How did the audience respond to you and your speech? _____

_____

_____

Write any other comments you may have here: _____

_____

Self-Analysis

Speech Topic: _____

It is always a good idea to evaluate yourself after you speak. Answer these questions <u>after</u> you have delivered your speech in class. Going through this self-analysis will help to build your confidence and competence as a speaker.

How did your preparation affect your speech performance? Could you have been more prepared? _____

_____

_____

I think that my greatest strength during this speech was: _____

_____

_____

The one speaking skill that I can most improve upon is: _____

_____

_____

How can you continue to improve as a speaker? _____

_____

_____

How did the audience respond to you and your speech? _____

_____

_____

Write any other comments you may have here: _____

_____